PRAISE FOR STACY DYSON

Your poetry is like thunder and lightning and all that it's like to be a woman. Thank you for sharing your soul in words.

— *Mytrae Meliana, author of BROWN SKIN GIRL*

Testimony: Stacy Ardis Dyson is all artist, all the time.

— *Vogue Robinson , 2nd Poet Laureate of Clark County, author of VOGUE 3:16*

Her commitment to the evolution of literary scholarship is a marvel in and of itself. She pushes boundaries, dares to speak the unspoken, and never ceases to create anew. Of all my living poetic heroines, Ms. Dyson is unparalleled.

— *Kyla Rae Walstad, Social Tribe Media & Marketing*

My friend Stacy is a poet warrior. She speaks truth.

— *Chelle A. Carter –Wilson Author/Writer at Redbud Writers Guild*

If you believe in the power of poetry to move people and to start revolutions then check out my dear friend Stacy Ardis Dyson. She's a powerhouse! Beautiful words, beautiful soul, beautiful friend.

— *Rob Williams, Assistant Professor of English at Skyline College*

One of my personal poet-hero-warrior women. Thank you, Stacy, for helping me remember why I breathe--

— Marie Jenna, *Page to Stage: Women's Words*

She shines like the sun. I never seen anyone ever hustle poetry like her. To listen to her is bliss to your ears and soothing to the mind and the soul. To learn from her is a blessing.

— Jodi Allen, *vocalist*

She is meticulous, well-versed in the flow and construction of poetry that carries a distinct message and stands as an excellent example of African-American expression of how the community, in particular women, negotiate a society and a world that does not always accord them respect and place.--

— Rebecca Romani, *editor, freelance writer/producer, curator*

She has consistently chosen the tough path of serving her art and bringing it to others over the more financially secure paths she might have chosen. I admire her more than I can say for owning her gifts and choosing to go where they lead her. Those gifts have led her through the dark places of this past year. The protests that swelled with the deaths of so many Black people, the political attacks on Black women as they exerted their strength and power through the elections, and her own memories — all of this led to poetry she needed to write and we needed to hear. As a writer, I have some idea of what it takes to put words to the feelings and thoughts provoked by the world around us. As a white woman I needed to let her words cut through my layers of comfort and assumptions that being a white affords me. I am grateful

— ELIZABETH MARRO, AUTHOR OF CASUALTIES, A NOVEL,
PUBLISHER OF SPARK

LOVELY AND SUFFERING

STACY DYSON

For Julia,
who is
worthy of the
dream.

Love,
[signature]

CONTENTS

FOREWORD

I could go on and on about this pandemic...but I won't. We're still living it, in so many ways. So, let's not dwell on the obvious.

What I will say is that this past year challenged, pushed, bent me to a breaking-point. Baptized me in fire, blood, and a lot of truths about this country I wasn't ready for/ didn't want to face. I didn't break, but, oh, Lord, I came so close so many times.

I discovered my faith was stronger than I'd known. I found a voice that knew I had been bottling up too much for too long. That voice remains...and daily scares the Hell out of me. But that's okay when you can hear the angels cheering you on the other side.

I felt places in my soul that must have been there before; I simply hadn't named them. They kidnap my dreams, now, and celebrate their presence in every word I write/have written for this last year.

Welcome to my pandemic year—March 15/2020-March 15/2021. And feel free to shout/ cry/ signify when you find yourself in these pages. Because we are truly all in this one together.

Je t'aime — Stacy

1

IN THE BEGINNING

No, we can't talk about this/ not now/ not today/ not at this level of pain/ not in this level of pain and anger/ not in this pain and anger that is trying to break us/ trying/ maybe later/ maybe/ we just need to walk through the world for a minute/ until we can feel clear/ find heart/ breathe/ again.

DEFINITIVE

We don't care what you think/ the time is past/ for your opinion of how our lives should be lived/

we don't care what/ you think we should do or what should have been done/ the hour has long been gone since your approval or understanding of our movements interests us/

no/we will not talk about this/ because when we wanted to talk/ you did not deem it the proper time/ for conversation/ our voices/ realizations/ our thoughts and actions belong to us/

the lines have been drawn in the sand and in time/ your days of approving/ understanding/ weighing in on the tools we are given/ are over/ it will only be said this last time/ there will be no repetition or welcome for those who do not pay heed/

walk beside me/

or stay off of my path.

3

PLEASE STOP

Don't tell me you understand how I feel/ because you don't/

you can't/

you never will/

Don't tell me you wish you could do something/

(don't wish/ just work)

don't tell me you wish you could know how it feels/

No/

you don't/

I would never wish the way I feel right now on anyone/ anyway/

to grieve and burn simultaneously/ to burn/ choke/ cry/ repeat/ to feel as if the marrow of every bone had the blood boiled out/ then thrown away/ feel as if all the air has been stripped from the atmosphere and everything you have known or trusted your whole life?

Well-meant/ I know/

but those wishes are for you/ not me/

Stop/

Don't wish/

Honor their names/ honor their lives /

Don't wish/

Work/

and /keep moving.

RISING (LYRIC ONE)

You forbade us speak our language/ so we sang/

you stole/ then sold our music/ then took credit for the crumbs you gave in payment/

you tried/ to turn our poetry into street music that hustled your ideas/ we innovated all new rhythms/ you claimed kinship because there was money to be made/

our voices now cannot be duplicated/ thieved/ sold to the highest bidder/ your cash cow is dead/

the phoenix rising from its ashes/ will not recognize/ does not know you/ she never will.

AN OLD WISDOM

When an old wisdom beckons and holds your hand/

when an old/ wrong belief/ writhes and dies in pain/

by the time an ancient truth screams/ to birth a present reality/ in the storm of mad voices/ betrayed lives/ risk that is intoxication/

when seeds sown the forever before your birth/ claim root/ claim space/ then bloom with no season to bind them/

that is when you will know/

the new day.

6

LAST CALL

Know this

I have no investment in caring if you understand

KNOW this

my life mattered before you acknowledged the fact

my life mattered before you gave it your blessing

our lives were never intended for your nod of approval

we have stopped listening for your applause/ affirmation/ cries of
solidarity/

whether we have those tools or not/ we thrive/ persist/warrior on

your approval is the lace napkin at a barbecue

nice/ but not necessary

a good ally knows the value of silence

a fool demands attention for recognizing what has already been taught make your decision

then walk where I need your shield

or get gone.

RISING (LYRIC TWO)

The light/ sometimes comes in funny ways/ in the center of roses/ in sunlight on the star/ glancing off the edges of water bottles smashed by police/ mingling in the tears called forth by pepper spray/ sparkling along the blood trail from a rubber bullet to the face/ Real light though/ real light only shines in the hearts and minds of the righteous/ is only defined by the vibration of boots on the ground/ in the demand for justice/ sometimes the light/ comes in funny ways/ let it not be/ from gun-sights/ and the tips of swords.

TRUTH.STRAIGHT

I can't walk away from this/

can't treat it as intellectual exercise/ can't pick it up like a book before bedtime/

cannot/ will not sing/ scrub/ screw it into not being a fact/

there is no poetry to deny or erase the truth/ I am a Black woman/

I breathe stories that have yet to be sung/ I have and will continue to rock ev'ry body/ heart/ cradle on this planet/

You can bend/ shake/ heartbreak me/

or try/

into irrelevance/

what you will never do/ even in death/

is break me/

You did not provide me crown or wings/ you have not power to take them away.

9

NEGOTIATIONS

The white folk they run scared now/

found out Black folk no longer run hide beg /

scream in terror

We shout/ we march/ we catch you out

then tell the world

The white folk they don't know what to do/

they bluster- brag loud/ and nobody listen them

then they want to call name and threaten

the Black folk don't run hide scream/

beg in terror

. . .

We shout/ we march/ we demand

then tell the world

The white folk don't know what to do

they cry/ plead/ say sorry/

apologize with crocodile tears

The Black folk don't mammy/ hold hand/ coo "oh poor
one"/stroke hair

we laugh/ ruin their wallets/ take our dollars home

then tell the world

The white folk/ now/ they want to talk

they say/ "Listen/ we know how you feel"

"We need change/ We need conversation"/

this time

The Black folk say

"We don't wait for you/

can't hear such noise now/ no longer"

You hear US

Learn US

Know US

Understand? maybe yes/ no

we don't care/ don't run/ scream/ beg

through just surviving long enough/ to bleed more

No more shadows/ voices and swords

We set the time

state the terms bold/ loud/ sure

Then go/ and tell the world.

LOVELY AND SUFFERING (FOR JILLIAN CARTER GOFF)

I want to stop dreaming their names

I want to stop breathing their last words

I want to stop washing my hands for 20 seconds of "What's Goin' On" and "Precious Lord, Take My Hand"/ I want to stop sitting on conference calls/ numb/ or crying/ because another fake 911/ lynching/ murder/ was top news when I turned on my phone

I tell a lot of lies about allergies these days

I want to be able to call Breonna's name/ without aching and being sick/ crying for two hours

I need people to stop reminding me that Jesus was a rebel/ Jesus was a warrior/ keep my Savior's name out of your mouth/ if you cannot use it properly/ I am exhausted

in the search for just a bit more calm/ just a little more reason/ I am not out of patience/ I am finished being patient/ I am tired of warning you to learn the difference there is nothing more volatile/ than a Black woman who has made friends/ with both her beauty and her pain/ and we are lovely and suffering right now/ we are lovely and suffering right now

we are lovely and suffering/ RIGHT now.

SOME STORY

It was a weekday, I remember that

Daddy moved a little fast to beat the yellow- to- red

and lights started flashing about 30 seconds later

a motorcycle cop with his hand near his gun leaned in the window

demanded license/ lectured my father/

like he was a child

spoke to my daddy in a way that I had never heard any man address my
father

my bronze star/ purple hearts/ combat veteran father

my highly respected churchman/ deeply admired/ dapper-dan/

wicked smart

father

.   .   .

alone/

I know he would have hurt that white boy's feelings

but his daughter was in the car

and my father protected his girls at all costs

Daddy said

yes, sir/

I'm sorry, sir/

and bent his head

I don't think I had ever wanted to kill someone until then/

I absolutely wanted to spill blood right then/

but my father was in the car/

and I protected him at all costs/

so we both swallowed sick and angry/turned up the radio

neither of us said anything

about 20 minutes later, Daddy looked out the window

said /

"Normally, I would have... but with you here.../

I know, Daddy/

I know/

and we went on to other things

I have damned that cop a million times

for thinking he could make my father less

than/

I will love my father/ til long after I'm dead

for trusting me/ to see

just how much he loved me.

12

IN PLACE

I feel the need to preface this by saying I have no cause to complain

this is me saying I am home/ I am safe/ I am well-tended

but I am defiant and confined as a bird in a cage

and even if I escaped/ took to my wings

there are too few places in the world would welcome my landing

and I feel the need to process this

Today is not a good day/ I'm exhausted/ I'm worn/ on too many levels
to make sense or be cautious

tired of having my universe shrunk to a few spaces/ a day-out doctor's
visit once a month

tired of having to live my life at the whims of other people who only
care about themselves/ who revel in the fact that their ignorance is
willful endangerment

I am tired of missing my nephews and my friends/ my independence/ my autonomy/ my life

I am tired of white woman with cell phones who have too much time on their hands/ who figure that attempting a little murder will help the afternoon and ennui pass more quickly

tired of people who think signing their letters BLACK LIVES MATTER is all that is necessary to ensure the existence of/ three-quarters of the people on the planet/ that's right/ we stopped being a minority the day America carpentered its first auction block/

I am tired of leaders who play roulette with those who still believe in this country/tired of greed and demons lining their pockets with the lives of babies

I am all longing with no chance of sex/

passion that can only spend itself in one direction

anger that is sharp and forbidding enough to perform a surgery on the next idiot who crosses my path/ says the wrong thing/ looks through me the wrong way in the streams where I am trying to wash away some of my pain

to live this way/ it is wrong/ it is perverse/ it is what happens when plague and politics become intersectional/ when religion is called to quarrel with science/when there is no respite for body or heart no matter where or how you seek oasis

My hours melt into mass/ I have no signposts to create memories/

when all of existence is the same/ memories for good or ill require some definition of time/ there is not that now

And yet I know I am not truly suffering/ not as millions are suffering

my soul shakes/ is shaken/

that's all/

but today/

that is more than enough.

QUIETED SOUL

People always say that our ancestors/ are buried/ in our blood

we need to get away from that noise /

it is dangerous and untrue/

it implies that they lie coiled and sleeping/ waiting to be called

instead of telling the truth

that they spring up/ jump up/ dance

cry with us/ through us/

but do not run/ no/ they never run/

not unless it is toward the enemy/ armed with books/ and music/ and wisdom/ and faith/

a sword if need be/

they act as shield/ as prophet/ as second wind/

when the world has knocked the air out of you/ just/

for being Black/

or a woman/

or daring to love who you feel like/ need to/ love

they are on duty/ on call/ on point

the only time they sleep/

is when you are loved/ and singing/

when you are loved/ and in prayer/

when you are loved/ and smiling/ back/

at remembering what they gave/

you

weeping in sheer/ unbridled/ joy

at the thought/

because/ in those times/ they know

it is/ safe/

to rest.

NIGHTMARE FOR A SUNNY DAY

Here's the breakdown

I am not doing well/ just that/ I am not doing well/ fatigue and worry
have combined to deny my sleep/ I am nerves stretched to the point of
brittle resignation/

every shadow is a terror/ not a curiosity or adventure/ I am living in my
head because what lies outside is all chaos and uncertainty/ and the fact
that I cannot even voice that line without wanting to cry/ is certainly
more than I was born to bear

I have the consolation of not being torn/ the nausea and headaches exist
on the same plane/ there is no competition between them and my fear/
indeed/ they serve as a counterpoint to my anger

I am torn between hiding in some cold dark corner of my betrayed
heart/ or burning something down

anger not being an emotion in which I often strategy/ it is messy and
expensive/ there are more valuable things to do and be/ with my time

but I am living in a place/ right now/ where every bit of what I
believed/ was raised to believe/ is being violently murdered in front of

my eyes/ the prayers and beliefs that have protected me all my life are thin/ wrapped in rags and huddled close as shield against the firestorm

I don't think this is a judgement or punishment/ though it would not surprise me/ to be proved false

I do not think this is warning or visitation upon the sinful/ although in tradition of certain theologies/ that is how it would be defined

I don't know what this horror is/ or who it will take/ or how it will run

I do know it takes every strength I possess/ to use my faith as it's meant to be used/ and some days/ today/ that is simply/

not enough

I have not the energy nor inclination to be a warrior today/ to be strong today/ to function past simple survival/ there is no room for heroics or nobility/ I cannot even voice my opposition to another burden/ another disaster/ another demon living in my pocket/ I have no solution/

and I refuse to further tax/ a faith that is tempted to crumble under the weight of constant barrage/ I am in desperation/ in the struggle to keep my anger useful/ and focused/ selfless/ but today/ today is nausea/ headaches/ and fatigue/ the bad dreams are winning/

the bad dreams/ are winning.

KAREN, YOUR MAMMY DONE LEFT THE BUILDING (FOR BRENDA AGUIRRE)

Step 1

Make it ALL about you

Step 2

Do your best to justify your ignorance/ action/ lack thereof/ or faux pas

Step 3

Cry

It's supposed to make me feel bad

(I am so tired)

Step 4

Get defensive

Step 5

Self- deprecate (just a little)

Step 6

Cry again

let your voice go up half an octave

the sell will be stronger

not more convincing

just more noticeable

(I am SO tired)

After all

this is all about creating tension

and getting even MORE attention

RIGHT?

Step 7

Use the code words

"we're ALL sisters" "I DO support YOUR people"

"I am NOT a RACIST"

invoke the husband/ best friend/ former inamorata/ current partner

so that we know you have been liberal IN PUBLIC

and that makes it real

hence, only the Lord can judge you

Step 8

Keep up, now

look delicate and hurt

get that lip/ eyelash action going

voice quaver

aaand...

Step 9

Cry

(I am so tired

SO SO SO TIRED)

I am so tired

of white women's tears

and affirmations/ and denials/ and cries

of no substance

that cost you nothing

but a little cheap makeup and some stinging in your foot where you
stamped it too hard

Black and Brown girls get the taste of their own tears slapped out their
mouths on the quick

by mothers and aunties and grandmas who refuse to let us roll tongue
and savor what the world is ready to crucify us with

We don't display those tears for just anybody

which is why when you get a sistah to show them

you better get right and give your soul to the Lord

'cause it's about to get so deep you will most likely not be coming back

alive

. . .

We have long known those particular waters are rare resource

we don't use it up

we don't drag it out for everyday

y'all are wasteful

disrespectful and ignorant

splashing those tears about

wasting them on "NOBODY CARES" and "SHUT THAT NOISE UP"

I can't be a sister to somebody who cries over a word or an unfulfilled wish or evidence that she is weak and wrong and not getting her way

I can't be kin to someone who so carelessly weaponizes

what I had to bleed out

for the right to own

Step 10

Hear me

Hear US

hear the voice of every Black and Brown sister who has done time in person/ in emotion/ hearts operating on maybe

hearts we've had to patch with prayer

and pain

and promises

Step 10

HEAR US

Don't NOBODY care if y'all cry

My sisters and I are too busy using our handkerchiefs to bind the wounds of the world

We have neither time nor inclination

to wipe your face.

HOMAGE

I no longer keep a Bible/ by my bed/ I used to/ the one I had been saved with/ fragile/ onionskin pages/ lined in gold/ I read that book from cover to cover/knew psalms by heart/ and I have lived through enough to honor all of the commandments/

Tried not to go for broke/ been tempted to or seen others/ break/ most of them

I lost King James to a flood in Louisiana/ I admit it did grieve me/ some

But my other bibles survived/ part of my more-important-than my life – packet/ part of my "I-will-save-you-first-in-a-fire"/ or/ as it turned out/

flood/

Plays by Black Women/ An anthology of Black poets/ published 1971/

no thin and gold-leafed elegance there/

pages torn/ crumpled/ folded over/ marked with hair grease/ quick tears/ sweat/ and far too many memories for the voices to lie/ quiet in my hands

Those sistahs and brothers jump off their pages/in a flat-out running off at the mouth/ shouting their dreams at me/warning me not to get lazy or forget/

to do my job/ lest they die/

These folks made every word my own pen writes/ or will ever/ shaped explanations of my experience/ til I could write the definitions myself

they have/ literally/ survived flood/ and famine/ and fire/ in the form of hard times bitter choices/ and pain I could not regulate/

a relationship outlasted only by/ the one I have with God/ and love/ and the music we survive to/

They were not made to sit quiet in a pretty garden/ gazing at sun-dizzy petals/ nodding in the heat/

they were not meant to hold voice still/ be captive/

Telling me to step-star/ scream plain or fancy/ just get it done/ We came through Hell and fire for you/ the debt is not clear/ until you walk through/ AND make it to the other side/ alone/

I know / I/ do know/

But this is all I have right now/

Homage/

Give me time to gather/ new strength/ I will abandon the grace of flowers nodding in the heat/

and move to create battle-scarred pages/ of my own.

AUGUST 14:41

The butterflies begin their dance around 2:00

sometimes earlier if the sun is out in full force

I have actually (unfortunately)

spent time cataloging their habits

instead of working

they do not seem to like the cloudy days

The hummingbirds defend flowers too small to capture my attention

make any difference

they are sun worshippers, too

I guess

There is so little else to do

. . .

Not to be done

there is plenty to be done

finish edits, advertise workshops

try to not make today and all the others

feel like prison

a feeble cliche when the bars are sunlight, music, and dust-motes

I am trying to be sensible

The world outside is not safe for me right now

I am on the wrong side of the calendar for this

hobbled by a system that insists of attacking itself

I am bitterly resentful of losing autonomy/ independence/ days/ hours

parts of my heart and

on very bad days

what passes as my sanity

I was never one to deal gracefully with being trapped

small/ confined spaces only fascinate me when I know there is a
way out

there is not even the hint of a possibility of light

at the end of this tunnel

because we don't know where the tunnel is located/ supposed to
finish out

we just want a way away from all this

I try focusing on my work

It's hard to write between fear and ennui

worrying that every sneeze or throat ache signals something worse

I am tired of the smell of antibacterial soap on my fingers/ and not seeing/ my friends

I swear to God, when this is over

I am hugging total strangers at the coffee bar

smile when you give me change at the grocery

I will likely leap the counter and ravish you

Hold out a hand to help me through the door or off the plane

damn the scandal

we are making out on Concourse C

right in front of the

Build Your Own Burger stand

Dear God, how do people get through this?

I am trying/ working/ praying

being sensible

trying not to use my craft as crutch

that is not its function

I should be ashamed to even think that way

The theory is that you meet the challenge and take the change out in
bad dreams

my dreams are about all the things I miss most

meat/ men/ people

I can't get to or go see

I am trying to

not indulge in self-pity

I am struggling not to be maudlin

too many bird and butterfly garden days

are not good for me

make it too seductive to not get my work done

But reality right now

reality is full of fiercely hard edges and broken glass teased with
cyanide

I struggle to keep the taste of poison out of my mouth/ my heart/

my words

I am spared the journalist's mandate

I am a poet

and responsible for no truth but my own

It's a more difficult trick than one might imagine right now

I am trying to maintain some sort of balance

I am trying to stick to necessary stories and illuminations/circumstances and misdeed and heroines and honor and courage and paybacks/ dirty tricks/ big deceptions and small victories

My world is off course

and that is when I am called to be the most productive

But I cannot write about Breonna because to even think her name is an explosion in my brain and heart and spirit

and I need to be quiet in those places now so that my soul can heal from some of the battles I have bled for the last 3 years

recover from some of the pain visited on my naivete

the small excitements are beginning to wear my patience

I must be healing then

because I want to rise from my dreams screaming in triumph

I want to run/ singing.

BREONNA'S SONG (LYRIC I)

I am sorry, little sister

I had meant to call your name before now

but to even think it most days

was more pain than my heart could hear

made my pen shake like a fever in my hands

and today

the day 4 other mothers' Black girls

died in church

your mother was offered 12 million dollars

to wipe the tears off her face

and be quiet

12 million reasons to fold your memory into dust and an "on this day in history" headline

12 million ways of saying that material ease is fair and all one can really wish for

when your daughter has wakened just in time to watch her life breath

get ripped out of her throat

This is blood money, for committing murder and getting caught

30 pieces of silver to recognize

not apologize

12 million excuses from the police and their collaborators

12 million people who turned their backs and refused to listen to pleas for justice

(such a simple idea

and yet, it can never seem to be executed

not for us)

12 million throats raw with revenge/ bile/

disappointment in this place

choking

in an effort to not bring violence forward

so as to honor her name

with all but a sword

(But, mark this

that day is coming)

12 million tears shed by family, blood-tied or bonded

12 million tears for the lies and filth they want to shovel onto her name

so that we will doubt her, revile her

forget

(We are not going to forget)

12 million sleepless, pain-bright hours

haunting the mother who lived through being mother to a Black woman

(Raised her right/ did everything right

The way they tell us will protect our children

It doesn't. It's all a lie)

only to see her baby murdered in her sleep

It's only money

not life/ not time/ not joy or anticipation

It's only money

it means nothing

its sole purpose to pacify

Tell me

Exactly how do you calculate how many bloody drops are needed

until an innocent bleeds out?

How do you calculate how many thoughts fly through your head when you wake up just in time to breathe your very last?

This is not just compensation on any level

it is just

compensation

pacification

it is an insult to the memory of everything

Breonna was, Breonna was meant to be

I am sorry, little sister

I am so sorry

because the world is filled with people who will think "Well, that does it"

"That solves the problem"

I am so,

so sorry, little sister

Turns out your life was only worth

what Guilt had in its pocket today.

19

RECLAIMING OUT TIME (FOR RED MEDUSA)

My not-so-dear Sirs: On behalf of sisters everywhere

I am re-claiming the word "angry"

because we are not supposed to be

THAT thing

never mind what happens to us

never mind the insults thrown in our faces on every level/ every day

In the name of sisters everywhere

I want to reclaim the word "strong"

not used as it is now

not used as a weaponizing force

to undermine our vulnerabilities

simply an acknowledgement

that we can kill you 14 different ways with our tears/ or bent backs/ or open thighs

Yes, we will still be patient and long-suffering

just only in the way that you are patient and long-suffering/ when you are studying the enemy and ready to spill blood/ before nightfall/ before dawn

because we're supposed to be quiet and patient and strong

we are not supposed to be angry when you rape us/ betray us/ murder our children

cheat us in finance and government

you tell us/ expect us/ to lick your tears/ and be glad of the water

Every sister on this planet/ has done time at the altar of white/ male privilege

every sister on this planet/ has done time/ trying to hold her head up

while burying her heart/ in the dirt

(or having it torn/ to shreds/ and buried for her)

We are reclaiming it all

we are using the words as they are meant to be used

which means we are through listening

we are over conversation

past the indignity of letting other people define/ legislate/ social more/ condition us/ into any truth but the one/ REAL/ truth

In the name of every sister

in this place, on this planet

in the name of every sister/ been forced to breath deep and smile to keep her children/ her job/ her man/ her soul

intact/

I hereby reclaim our voices/

reclaim our space

claim/ encourage/ ride in bold/ on our anger

I hereby reclaim/

OUR TIME.

20

JE T'AIME

I survive by the grace of angels

(No, this is not one of those poems)

no hymns or hallelujahs

just statement of fact

I live in the grace of angels

it is the only way I have

been able to make a way

No fragile-bodied creatures

steeped in homage and holiness

not a one of them wears wings

(First of all, do you know how heavy feathers get in the rain?

Ain't nobody got time to go to the cleaners)

no, they wear classic, old-world names

Rebecca, Shane, Elizabeth, Jane

sisters who life-line me back

from the occasional hells of my life

and I love you all

not just because you love me

but because of your understanding

that work needs to be done world-wide

work we should all be doing

being strong, being kind

making change

that defines your divinity

'cause Jesus knows it's not your language

(some of that mouth could burn the black off midnight)

not your tempers

(Girl, y'all wanna talk mood swings?!)

not any of the traditional signs, airs, or graces

of Heaven's host

no, you ladies

(Now, I am aware that some or all of y'all object to/ hate that word. But this is my poem. So deal)

you ladies tend to this world and its troubles

with the effective, gentle, disciplined slash and thrust of a samurai's blade.

.   .   .

You cry, holler, drink, make art, raise hell and children, take lovers, and
Lord, did I mention the language?

you are champion at identifying need, making way out of no way

being strong, being kind, being effective

clothed in righteous belief, haloed with tears and hope

washed in the blood of the belief that things have to change

people have to stop hurting other people

people have to stop being hurt

You listen, you act, you laugh,

you hear

you've pulled me back a few times

from that rare and darkling edge

so that I could gather the space and time to remember

I had work to be about in this world

Rebecca, Shane, Elizabeth, Jane

thank you

for being the ladies (Yeah, I know. Get over it, already)

that wipe tears, cradle hearts,

and kick my butt

I remember who

I am

watching you be

loving, rowdy, effective, smart, mouthy, funny

Warriors

Yours are 4 of the names

I write across my daily devotions

because you refuse to leave a sister

(anyone, really)

bent, bleeding, and alone

Thank you for binding my wounds, restoring my voice,

pushing me not all that gently

out of the healing tents

to fight my way back

to where my life/ work lay dying

from lack of air and simple hope

Keep workin' your hustle, ladies

(I heard you the first time, okay? Damn)

go dance

do art, toss back your hair and another drink

hot-kiss your lovers, raise nine kinds of hell and strong children

. . .

And when the world is just that little bit too much on your heart,

in your head

weighting your shoulders

on those days where you can breathe just deeply enough to remember

how much you hurt sometimes

go sit down somewhere, please

Just

rest

Sleep

be still

knowing that so many people love you

(I

love you)

past all and any sense or reason

we exist, we breathe, we get better

because you

Are.

21

100 (FOR STACEY ABRAMS)

This was a conference some years back

he and I hit it off right away

laughed, rolled eyes, sent notes during the dull and boring parts

Every break, every lunch-time he was

right there

smiles and praise for the points I made

the conversations I held

my way, my words, my wit

Now, I'm not blind or egomaniacal

I know when I'm lighting and being delighted in

I know when I'm lit (not that way) and delighting

. . .

So, after the last meeting, I asked about a relationship

after running the checklist, of course

(no ring, no possessive exes, job, a good vocabulary, dressed nice, and
his mama lived eight states away)

For the first time that week

he stopped looking me in the eye

hemmed and hawed and then said

"You know, you're obviously intelligent

interesting, admirable

I'm flattered, truly.

But we can't date

'cause you're not a size 8".

He went on to repeat

"I'm flattered, really.

But I couldn't let my boys

see me with you.

It's well-known I like my consorts thinner.

But I like you, I really do."

The moral of the story?

This is why Stacey Abrams isn't vice-president

.   .   .

Nobody is talking about this but the sisters

and this sister is gonna break it down

so that even the folks in the back can understand

Stacey Abrams gave us the numbers to turn Georgia blue

800,00 votes

800,000 possibilities 800,0000 freedoms

800,000 voices of people that had been gerrymandered/ignored/ jim-
crowed into submission

never really considered useful or human

She gave us those numbers

but the only one number she got back

was 100

Not as kudo for the level of excellence achieved

not measurement of the gallons of bloodsweattears spilled/poured into
this campaign

not a count of the numbers of hours spent weekly making sure Georgia
did what we all needed/ pleaded/ begged it to do

No, it was the number of pounds they told her to lose

if she wanted to be seriously considered for second chair

.   .   .

Don't get me wrong, this is not a diatribe against thin women

light-skinned women

women with what my grandma used to call "good hair"

In the words of my street cousins "Girl, I ain't mad at you."

This is about a woman of accomplishment

of moment

of power

who, regardless of all that cred

is defined by her body shape

And yes, social politics say it's wrong

and 10 out of 10 folks asked will deny and take offense and say of course it doesn't matter

but that 100 has a lot to do with why Kamala Harris in the White House

instead of the woman who just literally helped save the free world

It's not as if we haven't been told

don't know better

let me run it for you again

we know the truths

.   .   .

Society has got to stop equating weight with morality

stop equating weight with beauty

stop equating weight with how effective or intelligent one is

Just

stop

And by the way

this social phenomenon is restricted almost exclusively to women

and zeros in on women of color

And now that we've brought it up

let's talk about the color of her skin

"Too dark", they whisper behind closed doors

"She's good for the field and the kitchens

but don't put her in the parlor

lest she scare the white folks away"

(and yes, that is exactly what that means)

Sis can't pass the blue-vein test

"blacker the berry, sweeter the juice" be damned

on the national stage, it's still

"if you dark black, get back"

to the kitchen/ to the field/ to the places where you might be heard

but can't be seen

They say "She's got that mammy look" (oh Lord, not the mammy look)

'cause in between that and her hair

(yes, her curly, natural, prob'ly-hard-to-deal-with-sometime hair)

she never had a chance

and last, but not least, the gap in her teeth

Now, in East Africa, that's considered a sign of luck

but here it's mostly seen as an embarrassment/ or a sign of poor
hygiene/ or neglectful parents/ or an impoverished childhood

or just poverty in general

which almost certainly signals a shaky moral compass

And you might be laughing, but there are studies showing that there are
people who equate poverty with less-than-sterling morality

The elephant in the tea-room is this country's ongoing love affair with
telling people

especially women people

how they need to look if they want to get anywhere

if they want to be seen

if they want to be valued or of value

.   .   .

That's supposed to have gone away by now

it hasn't

it didn't

it won't

This woman didn't just deliver an entire state to Biden on a silver platter

ribbons pressed and curled

she sent a message to that deposed idiot that said "Boy, you need to stay out of our house. Don't you EVER come back down to Georgia, 'cause the sisters are waitin' on you."

(for the uninformed, it is never a good thing to have the sisters waitin' on you)

But she is too fat, too black, too direct

destined to discomfit the white folks

So America will what America does—

use her (field hand)

take what she makes (house negro)

let her clean your messes

raise up your neglected children (mammy),

then lay up in the bed with her if you're desperate or it's convenient

. . .

But when it comes time to pay her back for her labor, brilliance, and dedication

when it comes time to pay your debt and give her the world she has earned

there's a lot of throat-clearing and because why and not looking anywhere but to down to the ground or up at the sky

Some worn and tired "let's give her roses now" stickers

and the dangling promise of a governorship (about which I have my doubts)

Yes, she is fascinating and yes, you're flattered

(Forget flattered. You should be on your knees in gratitude. This woman kept us out of certain Hell),

The praise will be more the praise you give a good servant

not an equal partner

the praise you give an asset

not a necessity

You like her, you like her a lot

But what would your "boys" say?

Let's be real...America and Stacey Abrams might dance

might flirt, might hook up for a minute

but it will never be anything more serious

forget a marriage

they can't even date

She's much too black

and she's not a size 8.

22

A LITTLE LYRIC (FOR YEMAYA)

Most of my work

has been my work in the world

what I was born to do

I'm a poet

I observe, I record, I tell truth

that's my job

but for the majority of this cursed and heart-breaking time

this insulting, impatient time

it has been only that thing

Work

. . .

There is no joy

little grace, less elegance

the truths I have to tell are not always pretty or pleasant

but so many of my hours are nothing but unyielding drudgery

and I did not get into this business

to feel this way

I did not choose to be a warrior

God called

I took heed and ran

toward light

as it is well documented

that you may tarry on The Spirit

but The Spirit is not gonna hang around waiting for you

and I was not raised to make my Savior wait

I understood it would not always be fancy and sun-bright syllables

even so

I could not have been meant

to hurt, to burn like this

all the time

24/7 should be a time measurement

not a death warrant

but everything has felt forever

in the worst way possible

and most of these rudely shattering days

I have no joy in what I was called to do

but this last reading

I sat and watched a sister in England

read her truth

and while she did

her daughter did everything she could to distract mama

(who was obviously not paying enough attention)

Yemaya tumbled on the bed, giggled,

sang, giggled louder and harder when mama told her "Hush!"

just had Mardi Gras while mama was singing her spirit

Now, let it be noted that I loathe distractions online

I will never think your cat is cute

ooh and aah over your dog's jaunty trickings

have been known to mutter (mic and camera safely off)

"Get that child in her bed, there are grown folk talking"

But this li'l-bit-brown-sugar-girl

had a laugh that lit a smile I hadn't worn all day

just a little, small moment of grace

tumbling, sliding, twinkling all sassy

while mama did her work

a beautiful li'l-bit-brown-sugar-girl

with absolutely no idea or care

about grownup, dismal hours

(please God she stays that way for long as can be)

And I wrote this poem to say "Thank you, Sugar-bit"

for shaking the pain away from my soul

for just

a minute

for reminding me that dire circumstance and evil times (like now)

are forever in the wind

but always

always

(somewhere/ sometime in the day)

at least one small and delicate delight is given

so you remember

give thanks

and level your breathing.

23

KAREN, YOUR MAMMY DONE LEFT THE BUILDING PART II

On a scale of 1-10

1 being

"Back away slowly from the cookout.

Nobody needs to get hurt."

and 10 being me offering physical violence to elders

as in I will slap your grandma and mine in the middle of Main Street at high noon for this

my irritation level is at about 45

and rising

All this crying and pearl-clutching got me in a

non-conciliatory frame of mind

miss me with that noise,

please

. . .

Why is my pain only validated by your distress?

When Black/ Brown women cry for their babies,

why is it necessary for white tears to validate the experience?

Is it because we've done it so often that our tears are invisible,

don't count anymore?

Why is any conversation always at your behest?

We've been wanting to talk for centuries now

Why are our lives suddenly worth taking notice?

Because you finally decided to take notice?

Well, then

must be important

Check it, one white woman got upset one morning

spilled her coffee, got national headlines, and changed the law

WE get up upset every morning, every hour of every day

spill all the tea

and get called gossips, abrasive

nasty and non-pleasing

I was raised up carefully

well-born and well-bred

so the most I can say to that is

you may personally kiss it right here

'cause F that S

(Yeah, go on and laugh, but I have ancestors to answer to)

(Sorry, Grandma)

Speaking for sistahs everywhere

keep our names out of your mouths

'cause in case you hadn't got the memo

whatever you start

we are going to finish

Don't waste your tears on

trying to impress us with your pain

we live where you only visit

and tourists, quite frankly, are not welcome

sisters bleed, bond, and back each other up

y'all want to eat the cake and not clean up the kitchen

then get upset when your dainty selves

catch hands or our ambitious dreams

without stopping to drink at the river of your

opinions

.   .   .

Some of y'all so weak

can't take a "Becky" between the eyes

can't get hit with the truth

without crying about your stress level

keep self-importantly screaming

"You're the one making it about race!"

(Well, yeah because it is.)

(It always has been.)

You want to call me sister?

Prove you fight like I do

that's right, you have to prove it

don't want to see your pink cat-hat or your Notorious RBG tee-shirt

Show me oppression turned into beauty marks,

like children with full bellies

and laws that protect everybody

Show me relationships full of truth,

not convenience

Show me your souls-tears hit the earth

and birth renewable energies

like gold

and water

and real love

You want me to call you sister?

Listen to me,

stop using me

celebrate who I am without

making me use your mirror

Back me up, honor and

sing my songs, too

Stop trying to be me when it suits or is fashionable

just be real

do you

And if that sounds like too much

well, let's put it this way

If after using my milk to suckle your children

after raising those children so they could sell or slave me and mine

after scrubbing your floors and your clothes

so you could go to fundraisers where I got talked about as "the problem"

after being given the back seat in movements I bled out over

after moving ahead as an exemplar of my sisters,

only to be judged by the standards by which the world celebrates everything you do or say or decide to be

If after all that

you decide we're ungrateful or impatient

or too angry

Ya know what?

You may personally, can unreservedly,

kiss it right here

'cause

F that S

(Sorry, Grandma).

24

BALLAD FOR MARISSA AND MIZ PALMER (AND ALL THE REST)

I was tired

of being threatened, of my children being threatened

of being in constant physical danger

all I did was fire a bullet into the ceiling

I never meant to hit him, I knew I wasn't going to

I hit what I aim at, okay?

For trying to protect my family I caught

20 years,

Did hard time

in lockdown

for being tired

. . .

I am tired

I sent my child to a better school for a better life

the judge handed me down five years

When another mother/ a celebrity mother/ a white mother

lied and paid somebody off so her child could be at the "good school"

she caught a two-week sentence at a country-club jail

walked out after 11 days

said she was sorry

I don't have enough money for my sorry to make a difference

I'm still in prison

and I'm tired

The level of fatigue we're dealing with right now?

This is something that Black and Brown women have known

all of our lives

we are past exhausted

with having to hold up half or more of the sky

hold family together, hold ourselves together

it becomes too much

and yet when we say we need our down time/ alone time/ self-care

time to mourn or create something

anything that is not for general consumption

we are told be strong sister/ you got a little bit more in you sister/ come on sister you can keep going

No

Why should I?

Why should I be required to?

We can't

we just can't

with y'all...men/ children/ the world

we just can't with y'all some days

estoy muy cansada

the lights are always on

we sleep in crowded ugly spaces

the woman next to me has wounds

from trying to keep her daughter

from being ripped out of her arms

she cries dark and ragged-edged stars

onto the gray floor

Yesterday, they took me to another ugly sterile space

to make sure I would never have children

I have wounds and bad dreams about vanished babies

the woman and I cry together now

I am so tired

past tired, really

I never sleep anymore

because my daughter slept

just long enough

to be executed by a hail of bullets

that had nothing to do with her

I don't know that I will ever sleep again

In the street they shout "say her name" "say her name"

I just whisper it into my heart

where I know she can still hear me

If you listen late at night/ early morning

whenever the world turns again

you hear them in every kind of cage there is

Mothers who cannot reach

their babies crying

and make rescue

the way mothers do

. . .

Mothers whose babies

grew, are growing

knowing mama tried to protect them

but could not protect herself

Mothers whose children defied the natural order of things

and died first

Mothers in tears/ in pain

who cannot sleep

Mothers in every kind of cage there is.

25

LESSON IN LYRIC AND LIES

I am trying to teach Hanah the history of music in this country, which means we have to start with slavery

with cries to God for mercy and a better place

with signal songs and the Underground Railroad

Hanah wanted to know if slaves ran away because they did something wrong

"Were they bad people? Then why were they running?"

Hanah is in the 4th grade

her school ignores Black History month,

apparently they do not find it relevant to a Christian education

I got sick-to-my-stomach upset, angry

but tried to answer

still needed to answer

I did what I could

but her parents should have done more

I did what her school should be required to do

I am so tired of people raising their children to not see color

in other words

not raising them to celebrate individuality, not to cherish and protect difference

I am tired of people lying to their children that we are all the same

it's not true, it's not fair

it's not what I'm been sick to my stomach

heartbroken over

since

this time last year

I am going to use the word "complicit" here

and that will make some of you angry

and some of you uncomfortable

but you are complicit in destroying any hope of Black America ever becoming part of America

when you feed that crap to your children

you are negating every struggle/ every tear/ every ounce of blood spilled

in trying to make a way to acceptance

for anyone person of color/ any one Black person/ any indigenous person

who lives by their wits and through the souls and stories of our ancestors

the only thing that has kept us alive until now

We should all be the same legally

yes

all given the same opportunities

yes

all guaranteed equal and just treatment in every avenue every aspect of life

but making us one angered and unwieldly lump of homogeneity does nothing

but make life easier for you

keeps away the discomfort

allows you to walk through life ignoring the reality of things

you are in service to a broken and lying ideal

not the education of your children

and it should not be my job to do your job

If you don't see color

you don't see me

if you don't see differences, you are dismissing the lives and realities of three-quarters of the planet

. . .

If you cannot open your heart and throat at the same time to
acknowledge that I am not the same as you and your family/ ancestors/
lifestyle/ dream of the perfect place

you are not just in denial

you are spitting in the face of every child jailed

every woman raped

every man swinging from the closest tree branch

in the name of a promise of equality

You are a liar

and a dangerous one at that

because you teach those lies to your children

and walk away thinking you have done a good thing

when all you have done is teach them that their comfort level is more
important than the truth

Fire marked the sky near Hanah's house last year

protestors voices rang over and through night-wind

I am truly glad that she and her family are safe

that her parents kept her and her brother inside

the streets were no place for anyone's children that night

But I wish they had taken the time to stand in their yard

see the flames, hear the voices

then explain that the smoke in the air would linger

because Black people were being murdered for no reason

explained that the world is not fair or equal

explained that everyone should be treated the same

but is not the same

that everyone should see color, respect differences

I wish they had done a better job

so that I wouldn't be doing that job again

now.

26

MAMSELLE DES NEIGES (FOR NATE ABAURREA)

Yes, I'll confess I did it

I guess I should feel bad

I pointed out an obvious truth

and made a snowflake sad

I guess I should repent my ways

give my evil heart goodbye

but the devil was riding my shoulders

so I made a snowflake cry

All I did was point out that

her woman's day celebration

billed "international" was missing something

vital in translation

one woman of color, the rest were white

and not one lives abroad

so I pointed out the problem

with this visual monologue

I did not yell or scream "J'accuse!"

I did not show vexation

except to post on Facebook that I needed explanation

"Could someone please explain?", I wrote

I did not mention names

I did not say who'd made the call should walk a walk of shame

I sent a private message

I said I had concerns

poor snowflake's soul began to melt

and I got this return

I was unfair and she was hurt

she'd done her very best

one could almost see the tiny tears

drip onto her avatars' breast

Girl, keep those weepin's to yourself

I did not call your name

I didn't tag your venue

or advertise your shame

you were wrong, I called you out

in the nicest possible way

you don't get to be hurt, Babes,

you messed up

no matter what you say

But t'is ever the case with snowflakes

they hurt and melt and cry

when they get fronted with a truth

they simply can't deny

See, polar caps are melting

it'll keep on getting hot

you'd be safer to just say truth

than defending what is not

righteous anger doesn't play that well

where no righteousness exists

you screwed up

admit it, fix it

move on

don't stupidly persist

And when my wicked life is done

I'll answer to Pete on high

'bout how and what I've done whilst here

on our marble in the sky

I'll be proud to say I did mostly good

folk went low, I tried to go high

but one of the best things I ever did

was make a snowflake cry.

BREONNA'S SONG (LYRIC II)

27 erased by 8

equals blood on Daniel Cameron's hands

27 erased by 8

equals no more dreaming and still no justice

even now

27 erased by 8 only equals

more struggle and rest in power

and I know that mothers' tears falling century down century did not keep you safe

I am sorry that our soft voices and white gloved hands and choir singing were not enough to keep your safe

sorry that trying to fit into this tapestry

sacrificing to fit into this supposed sweet and welcoming tapestry

was not enough

our not being angry was not enough to keep you breathing

and I don't know what you had planned for your birthday

but I do know that you were a woman

not a symbol

I know that sometime you must have fussed with your hair

fussed at your man

fussed about your job

got loud with your girls, got out in the street

singin' and swingin' and blingin'

so you could forget about your day

laid up in the bed some days

watching the rain

made love/ made plans

I know that as a Black woman there were some days you couldn't take
it anymore/ felt like you couldn't see one more horror

but you stayed in the game/ went back the next day/ did your job

there were days when you just got tired of being a Black woman

. . .

Because that's what Black women do

that's what and who we are

we did everything we were supposed to/ we trusted and prayed and held our heads up and made way out of no way

we took it

we worked with it

we held on/ held it down

did the work

held it down/ held it together

held on and on and on

while this country/ this place/ did every wicked thing it could

to tear us apart

we did everything we could

used everyway we know

everyday and night living the way we are supposed to live to save our children

and it still wasn't enough

Our holding it down/ fighting the system/ setting streets on fire

soft words/ bowed heads/ white gloves/ swallowed humiliations/ and words and tears and songs and suffering wasn't enough

the way we have been told we need to live our entire lives wasn't
enough

You were still not safe

You were our daughter/ our auntie/ our little sister

(no, not our mother. Never anyone's mother)

we tried everything

you died anyway

right now you are on your way to becoming an icon

your name will go down as a martyr to the cause

I am truly sorry for that

because no one deserves such a hellish honor

27 erased by eight should not equal political expedience/ coverups/
lies/

does not justify or explain the dirt they tried to bury you with

27 erased by eight and wrong and a mother who will never sleep again

because her baby sleeps too young and forever

Why?

For what?

all she wanted

all anyone ever wants to be

is human

flawed and free and human

flawed and alive and free

to be human.

28

KAREN, YOUR MAMMY DONE LEFT THE BUILDING...FINI (YES, FOR BRENDA AGUIRRE)

I am reading my fifth story (this week)

about some Anglo chick who lost her shit

showed her drawers (as my southern cousins used to say)

and went live on a sister in public

then got all puddled up when she got called

on aforementioned shit

She apologized

we laughed

and she got mad again

I mean, for real y'all

Sistahs got things to do

your salt water machinations/manipulations

have ceased to be an object of pity

or interest

and the fact that we no longer give half a damn

really has you up in arms

But I do want to pause and give a shout out

to the incredible amount of energy it must take

to be your dainty and breakable selves these days

in between the fragility, weaponizing tears, and the tone-policing

you wonder when white women have time for anything else

It must be exhausting

all that running from imagined slights and/ or the truth

all that actually having to behave like an ally

(I said behave like one, not be one)

so that you can make your daily/ weekly/ hourly proclamations about the level of your wokeness

must have you bending deep and gasping for air

Tell me

what kind of tennies y'all use?

'Cause my true allies, all my sistergirls

been digging in bare heels

bare hands, bared breasts and hearts

to delay/ clean up/ escape the mess

you leave in your wake

those tears just leave a slick-n-nasty for us to breaks our hearts on

But I understand

when one is fatigued, one cuts corners

after all, the goal is the finish line

where you can be cautiously/ carefully handled

wrapped in old lace and cotton wool for the rest of your life

promising the same for your daughters

I know y'all are tired

poor things

having to slog through being told "be honest or be quiet"

having to make your way through having to make account of your actions

Well, no orange slices and water from us

no comforting bosoms upon which to lay your misunderstood and addled heads

no iron tablets or pep-talks

.   .   .

Your tears and tantrums, your "so I can seem correct" non-apologia

stopped being important or taken seriously

as soon as this country ripped apart our wounds and

made us wash in the corrupted, filthy blood

made us stir our tears into tea

that you thieved and drank

declaring the thirst to be equal, declaring that we would all drink the same

"Because sisters share"

You're right, we do

You don't

(selfishness is exhausting, too)

But we know y'all are tired

what with calling the cops/ making complaints/ asking for the manager/ telling us to be quiet/telling us not to cry/ getting in your ally points (just 10,000 more and you get a blender)!

so we'll just be getting on

Gonna pack some lunch

pack our shit

and git

. . .

We will not be returning to hold hands and wipe noses

ever

Because (for the last time)

Karen

your mammy done left the building

Y'all take care

And get some rest

Hear?

29

LATHER UP

There was no running to sterilize/ isolate/ wash your hands wash your hands wash your hands

when the AIDS virus swept through Africa and threatened to decimate an entire people

Where was all this concern for cleanliness when the Coen family flooded the ghetto with opioids?

Because that didn't become important until white people were affected

and then it became a crisis of mass proportion

You think DARE and "just say no" would have been in effect had it just been

Freddie who was dead?

Naw, Chad and Muffy had to shoot/ pop/ sniff/

before it got to be an issue

Let me tell you what

if this Covid only affected Black and Brown people

you wouldn't be hearing anything about it

except for a whisper of

"You see what these people bring in when you let them in"

A handful of nauseatingly woke celebrities

might throw us a telethon or cut a song

you could play over and over again on Spotify

If this Covid only affected white folk

there would have been a cure in the first

Two weeks

as it is, where do you think the trailers for vaccine volunteers are popping up?

Well, where do you traditionally find a guinea pig?

On a wheel in a cage

rootling happily through shit in the shavings

and only occasionally biting the hand that feeds him

One of my friends posted "wash like you're shaking hands

with the president"

Girl, please

First of all, I do not acknowledge fantasy

We don't have one of those right now

If I ever did have to touch hand with the jackal currently in power

I would require a full body bleach scrub and ritual burning afterward they don't make Clorox that strong or fire that hot

The hypocrisy of this mandate for cleanliness and care

chokes me so hard there should be fingerprints on my vocal chords

44 million dead worldwide as of right now

27 thousand and more here in the US as of right now

How hard is this to understand?

We are dying due to me first/ me only/ not my problem

because my grandmother is fine and my baby did not die last week

(but somebody's did...somebody's grandma died, somebody lost their baby)

How does that not hurt you?

How does that not threaten to break your faith?

I still have mine...my faith

But I have quarantined for the last eight months

in recognition of the fact that this is not just my problem

imprisoned by the fact that because I am Black (or Brown or poor)

I'm not important enough/ not Republican enough/ can't make any money for you enough

for you to wear a mask and

wash your hands

It hasn't affected you

it's just a cause to complain/ whine about inconvenience

whine about a liberty and rights that are not actually being threatened

We're not important enough

We're just not important enough for you to wash your hands

Wash your hands wash your hands

unless you're washing them

Of our lives.

30

LOCKED IN

I'm not quite sure

how much longer I can do this

the vaccine is here, but not available to me

not yet

I'm not old enough

I can wait my turn, sure

but it's been a year of isolation and bad dreams and tears over being trapped

I'm not sure how much longer I can wait

Outwardly, nothing suffers

I have been writing, I have been singing

but my focus is gone

reading has become an assignment

rather than a delicious assignation

I sing because I can't bear the silence of my autonomy being gone

forced cheer is no cheer at all

I have brave-faced more times than I can count

because I was afraid that one more day with a face mirroring how I really felt

would worry my housemates

to the point of "can we talk about it"

and I can't...I just can't

with anyone

not in anyway that makes sense

I tell friends I am "feeling my confinement"

and leave it at that

they understand the signal, and leave me alone

and I have to start singing again to fill the air with something

anything

There is something called locked-in syndrome

you are completely conscious, but completely paralyzed

there is no known cure

my worst nightmare has always been to be trapped

confined with no way out

no possibility of release

.　.　.

I grant you, this nightmare is prettier than most

sunny days and a butterfly garden

a whole summer lounging on the patio

which is only idyllic when you have a choice to go away

a chance to go away

somewhere anywhere

somewhere anywhere

somewhere anywhere I am not monitored or having to monitor

washing hands and wearing masks

and measured off spaces of safety

it breaks my heart in more ways than I can bear

to know there is no place in the world

where I could live unconcerned by even minuscule safeties

I am going to have to start singing again

The air in this space is too thick with work I haven't done

and I can feel my whole self trying to make an escape

feel my whole spirit rebelling against one more day

of just one more day

Deep breath, take deep breath

time for something routine

a routine that anchors me to

a reduced reality

a quick, brisk walk inside the confines of

my confinement

and then

unfortunately

I will have to sing again.

31

DIRECTIVE

I keep hearing "We should have that conversation"

"We need to have that conversation"

"We should open that conversation"

I don't remember y'all wanting to chit-chat

when Emmett Till was murdered

by a white woman who later recanted

it was decades too late; the damage had long been done

and her apology fell on not only deaf

but unbelieving ears

Where was all this need to hold salon

when dogs, fire hoses, and jim crow ran

free in the streets?

Y'all talked about us, but you never talked with us

You made decisions based on what you would have done and how
you felt

the usual father/ master/ your betters know best

approach

Where was all of this rush and haste for dialogue

when the First Nations were murdered, displaced, and slandered to
make stealing their birthright seem God's will?

The Trail of Tears should be a scream in every history book

not some careless, barely noted whisper

Where was all this need for word-play

when Japanese-Americans

lost lifetime dreams and their children

because paying taxes and dying in loyalty to this place was not enough

to be thought citizens of this place?

Where was all this need for conversation when we were begging/
striking/ marching/ bleeding

to be included

in the conversation?

.   .   .

I don't think y'all get it

We have been excluded from talking for so long
that now
(just because you feel it's time to open a dialogue)
you get mad when we don't want to talk to you

When we wanted your attention
we couldn't get it
when we are literally dying to talk about this
you don't have/ need to stage-manage the time
when we want to explore possibilities
you either tell us to be happy with what we have
or what you would do in our place
(you are not/ never will be/ in our place)
and to back up/ shut up/ sit down

But once it affects you
you want to converse
you want to narrative
you want to have coffee and
discuss/ discuss/ discuss

.   .   .

Let me....let me....(Lord, let me calm down...

maybe not)

Let me make something burningly clear

Do you understand that white solutions to Black and Brown problems
will get us killed?

Shut your mouth/ let me say that again

white solutions to Black and Brown problems will get us killed

Turn off your opinions, open your ears

get used to the idea that we have thoughts

and minds and solutions of our own

a way we are forced to navigate through the world

that has to be acknowledged

Why don't y'all just talk amongst yourselves

while we get the work done?

Talk amongst yourselves

try solving the problems you created

Stop preaching and pacifying

we're not children and church is over

. . .

Do you live here? No? Well, here's the protocol

If you're coming to our house to learn,

Welcome

Take a chair/ pour a beverage/ mind your manners

if you're coming to instruct/ insist/ demand (the way too many of
y'all do)

if you are coming to make decisions for people with a voice and a will
of their own

Stay home

lest we beat you to death with the table

you think you're entitled to sit down at.

32

FOR TRAYVON MARTIN (AND ALL OF US)

We are the people who have been urged to prayer time and again/

We are the people whose labors for this country/

are drowned in the blood of

slavery/ race laws/ and the tyranny of privilege/

then reviled for raising our voices in protest/

We are the people whose lives/ were given us by/

the deaths of people/ who only wanted to make a way/ for their

children/ for themselves/

We are the people who /

no matter the windstorm of violence meted us/

are forever urged to think and pray and act calmly/

when no thought/ or prayer/ or calm /

was/ is/ has ever/

been spared/ in the way we have been betrayed/

nor justice/

nor mercy/

But even as we shake in righteous anger/

we pray/

labor forward/ move/ forward/

continue to teach our children to dream/ to believe/

to always do more than simply exist/

past what we are given/ or told/ or taught/

We continue to create ourselves/ the world this world should be/

because we know/ no other way/

because we know our worth/

because through all else/ we remind ourselves /

that the power of our souls and hearts overpowers all/

else/

We are the people/

and that single truth/

will save us all.

33

THE WORST OF TIMES

Let's start with the nightmares

I mean, we've all had them

dreams where all and everything is lost

home, family, way of life

those have been the nocturnal terrors of nearly everyone

this year

but what you need to understand

is how much worse it has been for Black people

for people of color

thorns that pricked your sleeping

felt like nails pounded into our flesh

nightly crucifixions

and to be honest

the pain wasn't any better when we woke up

Let's start with the trauma

of waking up every morning checking the news

scanning Google

to see whether or not the 13th amendment had been repealed

Do you think I'm kidding?

Yes, that was a real worry

You saw the last 4 years, you know it could have happened

It was on my doorstep to the point where a friend wrote and
congratulated me on living with someone who would hide me

would pass me of as a servant, if need be

Yes, it got to THAT point

Let's talk about fact

that whatever faith, whatever fictions I held about

this country

were destroyed

A slow disintegration at first

then uncaringly ripped away by people who really

don't see me as anything more than something to be

worked/ raped/ sold/ experimented on

in truth, it was no different than the history of this country

just glaringly plain and out in the open

. . .

The last 4 years were one slow and agonizing game of

Made you look

Made you cry

Made you bleed

I have never in my life

waked up in tears

gone to bed in tears

knowing that there was no respite in sleep

noting that whatever I woke to

was going to be so much worse than

what had numbed me enough to lose consciousness the night before

Let's look at the damage done

no, not yet

we're not there yet

the healing from this

will not come in my lifetime

the pain compounded by injury from

centuries past

the thought, the knowledge that everything I tried to believe

everything I bled to believe

betrayed me

betrayed people like me

I will sleep with that for the rest of my life

I will rise to that for the rest of my life

Having to know that, face that

Let's talk about the nightmares.

34

WHERE WERE YOU?

I joyfully scissor the list

once a year

on Facebook

I cheerily announce

"Great De-friending Eve is tomorrow. I am SO excited"

the sift and winnow ever so joyously occupies the next day

people who have stopped reaching out

people I don't remember

people who have straight pissed me off

it's a clearing out

like burning old love letters or updating your little black book

a few times a year, I definitively post

"I am busily engaged in not giving a lavender scented shit about certain people today.

If you think your name is on that list, it probably is"

and leave folk to figure it out

but in the last four years

I have had to let go

of people I used to love

people I heard close to my heart

people I let in my life

because I found out, rather,

figured out

I didn't want them anywhere near who I am

Not old lovers

that's easy

old lovers only break your heart

you broke my faith in who you were

it is not the same thing

I disappeared you deliberately

and destroyed any avenue back into my existence

the last years and this pandemic

made sure I knew who loved me

not the (as it turns out) mistaken image of me

You feel angry and upset and betrayed

I don't care

because there was one simple question none of you could answer

Where were you ?

Not a word when the streets exploded

I lived in agony, in terror,

Death on every level was running rampant in every city

and daring me to come out and play

Not a word when I rose and lay down and lived every single hour in tears and terror

Where were you?

my heart was so twisted by Breonna Taylor that I couldn't breathe right

I had days when I woke up worrying that slavery was going to make a comeback

days I walked stooped low, moving fast as I could

because I felt like a target was painted on my back

. . .

You called me friend and sister and saw people who looked like me being murdered and caged and actively told that our only right in this country was to suffer

that we should be damned glad of any attention at all

you saw what this country was doing to the ones who literally built and maintained this country

Where the Hell were you?

You were complaining

about how the women and children you housed weren't grateful enough to you

about not understanding why I was so upset of photo ops you sent me

with Melania Trump surrounded by Black children and Brown orphans

You were condescendingly telling me how naïve I was

to believe that an Hispanic mother with three small children who had never before been in this country, who had never even seen an elevator

couldn't navigate her way around two major airports in strange cities

You said there would be lots of people who spoke Spanish, lots of space for the kids to play

pointing out that there were plenty of benches where they could rest for 16 hours

You were busy asking me about stupid trivia on Kamala Harris and curtains

I stayed civil, voice low and reasoning

I ran interference and token patrol at the same time

so you could feel relevant and woke

I will own that bad

I did it far longer than I should have

And when I got tired of that role

when I snapped

you got your feelings hurt

You were wounded by the fact that I was barely hanging on some days

and it was reflected in my voice and manner of address

I was isolated, breaking

bleeding out any belief I'd had or held in what this country was
supposed to be

haunted by the obscenity of people dying without being able to see
loved ones

terrified that people I loved would die without me being able to say
goodbye

afraid I would die

And all you could focus on was how I wasn't the same

I wasn't consistent, I wasn't trying to be nice, be upbeat

What actually happened

was I stopped being your available negro

. . .

Right now, I am carrying so much anger that I am literally sick

my stomach in knots, ready to throw up

and that is on you

and the ones like you who do not understand

that I owe you nothing

I walk through this world so much differently than you do or ever will

I will not be bothered to explain that to you, nor should I be

I've tried to explain it too many times before

then, you only listened long enough to respond

not feel or think

Do I miss you?

Sure

but you're fading like all the ghosts in my life

The ones who truly hold my heart

stand 'round me strong enough

so that I will heal

quite well enough

and very, very soon.

35

CERTAIN MAGIC

This is no certain magic

In fairy tales,

the wizard casts his spell and the

hero triumphs

the maiden wakes from her years of sleep

all is fresh and renewed and

as if before

never happened

None of that is real

and this is not pessimism

simply the truth

which is not something people want to hear right now

they want to hear that the vaccine is wizard

that all will be as it was before

but that can never be

This is a possibility

not a solution

a progress

not a reality

at best, it is a cautious optimism

at worst

it is hope

The most evil and damaging thing you can promise someone

is hope in a new forever

this is life

and life doesn't work that way

A year ago

I woke up to find the world

my world

had stopped existing

autonomy, independence

the way I've managed and lived

all disappeared by something we couldn't even identify

I watched millions die for lack of understanding this thing

I watched friends mourn in a way no one should have to

mourn without the release of being able to say goodbye

I have thanked God nightly that my parents died before this horror

I have cried nightly because I might

add to that desperation of anguish

Seeing people who look like me

murdered on an almost daily basis

every day a new shooting

every day a new atrocity

every day a new shattering of belief

every single day having the innocence of my upbringing ripped raw
and quivering from my soul

Did you ever have something lying so hard on your heart

that you were fairly sure that to acknowledge it would break you?

I had to explain

(well, confess) to a colleague the other day

that everything I thought, everything I was brought up to believe

everything I have always believed

was no longer true

. . .

And I never thought that I would have to say this

to any living person

I never thought I would need to explain how so much of the way
you've lived your life

can break your heart

And it almost broke me (not quite, almost)

in between the tears and the heart-clenching

I thought for sure I was having an attack of some sort

I was

but it was on my spirit

not anything pumping lifes-blood

It was bad enough in the first two years

I kept thinking "it can't get any worse than this"

but every morning, every afternoon

every blessed night, it was always something new

some brand-new horror seemingly designed

to break the world, to break me

Let me go back to the beginning

I grew up believing three things

That people are basically good

That prayer will see you through

That this country, regardless of its myriad faults

would not forever (damagingly)

be blind

to the evils of ignorance, the greed of racism

the obscenity of willfully disenfranchising millions of people based on
no more

than melanin and an undeserved (but hard fought for) sense of
entitlement

I really did believe that reason would solve anything

(I still do, to some extent)

but the last two years personally/ professionally/ world wide

have nearly disabused me of that notion

as I told my colleague, there are only two sorts of people in the world

those who want to tease the band aid off, bit by cautious bit

so it doesn't sting as much

and those who rip the band aid off, damn the pain and consequences

The last two years proved the latter kind

everything I believed, everything I held dear

everything I had prayed on, wished on to be true

was ripped away from me, from my life

from the way that I thought

and that is a hard thing to accept

a hard way to exist

Torn, ripped away, and thrown into the gutters

every day, new blood

yet, people hail this new administration, these new medicines

as an end to all that is wrong and wicked

scream and sing and sigh in relief for getting back to normal

Normal was cold

uncaring

laden with guilt and selfishness

Normal was being murdered for being different

Normal was make it pretty make it dainty make it sweet

so that the smell of rot won't be an issue

Normal is dead

and not coming back

no matter how badly some must wish it

Normal cannot be allowed to start breathing again

that putrid, murdering breath

that breath that murdered innocent people and starved babies

cannot be allowed again

. . .

Hear this

what is coming is no true magic

it will require what great change has always required

work and sacrifice

work and hard choices

work and the courage to stand the pain of our innocence

being torn away from our protesting hearts

and thrown to lie trash in the gutters

No wizard's wand

no foretold kiss

This is no certain magic

Leave us to work

and build

and remember

so that Normal

does not happen again

that will be enough for now.

36

ESTA TERMINADO (IN HOPE)

My soul can be quiet now

it is finished, I have to move

have to, in Harriet's immortal phrase

go toward freedom or die

This pain, this anger, this confusion

have not gone

simply untangled and been seen to its proper place

I am ready to travel now

still burdened, but not as heavily

still deviled, but with not as many demons in my pocket

The wind has changed, the fever of the last four years has broken

I have been ill and uncertain

long enough

It is time for me to loose my worries

banish the wicked pain that created them

and make a way, make

my way

Home.

ACKNOWLEDGMENTS

This book belongs to:

THE SISTERGIRLS..who held me up, kicked my rear, let me cry, and refused to let me be broken

NATE ABAURREA...our weekly "poetry trades" anchored me in the tempest

STACEY ABRAMS AND REP. ALEXANDRIA OCASIO-CORTEZ...who define the words "warrior woman"

and

BREONNA TAYLOR...we got you, little sister. We got you.

ABOUT THE AUTHOR

Stacy Dyson is a poet, acapella vocalist, playwright who specializes in the life and times of the Black woman.

> Someone has to sing for my sisters. Their lives, loves, philosophy...There are centuries of stories begging to be told. I'm lucky enough to be one able to make those voices be heard.

Ms Dyson has done program design, residencies, workshops, and live performances in Colorado, Oklahoma, Massachusetts, New Mexico, South Dakota, Nebraska, Nevada, and all over San Diego.

> But the stage is my natural habitat. It's fine to tell your stories, but for me, unless I can vibe, interact with a crowd, my job is only half-done.

Author of seven collections of poetry (See Also By) are poems, stories and music that "celebrate/ document/ declare what it is for me to be a Black woman in this world, what it is to be an artist, how myself and my sisters navigate our lives. No, that way is not easy. But it is often joyous, and always carries the sanity of truth."

A former Poet Laureate for Imagination Celebration (Colorado Springs) a nominee for Poet Laureate for the State of Colorado. Founder/Lead Poet DragonsWing (Colorado Springs) and CoFounder/Lead Poet for Page to Stage:Women's Words (San Diego) she is also a Pikes Peak Community Foundation Individual Merit Award recipient, a Colorado Women's Playwriting Festival winner for her play FANNIE'S GIRLS: A 4-1-1 IN-5 PART ATTITUDE, and a TEDx speaker.

> It's never, ever about my single voice. So, the shows and women's workshops are extremely important to me. Especially now, our lives literally depend on knowing how to speak our truth, share our stories, bring thunder and healing with our voices. The workshops are women only because women will say and bring forth deeper parts of their souls when they're surrounded and supported by other women. I've heard stories, confessions,..
>
> Those conversations, those places have to be given due honor. They have to continue.

Currently, Stacy is promoting her newest collection of poetry FOLLOW ME ON THIS. Coming soon is AUGUST 5000, a play about sisters and their relationship, plus a new women's writing/performance workshop called FIRESCRIBE.

For further information on Stacy Dyson, her voice and vision: www.saintwinterraines.webs.com or www.wickedhotwords.com

ALSO BY STACY DYSON

Follow Me on This Coming soon

Author of seven collections of poetry:

- BLACK DIAMONDS
- OBSIDIAN ICE
- BLUES IN THE FIRST POSITION
- WOMAN 724365
- NEFERTIRI'S KISS
- POR INNOCENCIO
- and her latest, FOLLOW ME ON THIS

She has also created five CDs of poetry and spoken word.

- THE MADONNA OF NEVADA AVENUE
- POR INNOCENCIO
- A WOMAN BESIDE THE SUN
- SO MANY ANGELS
- and (Love Me) SAN DIEGO STYLE

Her poems, stories and music "celebrate/ document/ declare what it is for me to be a Black woman in this world, what it is to be an artist, how myself and my sisters navigate our lives. No, that way is not easy. But it is often joyous, and always carries the sanity of truth."

ABOUT RED THREAD PUBLISHING

Stories Change Lives

We believe in the power of women's voices & stories to change the world. We support women not only to write & publish their books but to really embrace their voice, accelerate empowerment & reach global impact. Because women matter.

Do you have a story that must be told? Sierra Melcher, author & founder of @RedThreadPublishing, & our team will support you every step of the way. www.redthreadbooks.com and info@redthreadbooks.com

CPSIA information can be obtained
at www.ICGtesting.com
Printed in the USA
FSHW011659200521
81668FS